SHORT WALKS
MADE EASY

SNOWDONIA

Ordnance Survey

Contents

Walk 1

THE GREAT ORME

Distance
3 miles / 4.9km

Time
1½ hours

GO BY CABLE CAR

Start/Finish
The Summit Complex

Parking LL30 2XF
Summit car park

Cafés/pubs
The Summit Complex

Exhilarating views, copper mines, cable cars and tramway

The Summit Complex

Park Farm

P V

Quarries

Page 14

Walk 2

AROUND CONWY

Distance
3.8 miles/6.1km

Time
2 hours

Start/Finish
Conwy Marina

Parking LL32 8GJ
Beacons car park

Cafés/pubs
Conwy Marina; Conwy

A fine sandy beach, sparkling riverside and historic town buildings

Walk 3

CAERNARFON TO PORT DINORWIC

Distance
4 miles/6.5 km

Time
2 hours

Start Caernarfon
Finish Port Dinorwic

Parking LL55 1TH
Shell Site car park

Cafés/pubs
Caernarfon; Y Felinheli; Port Dinorwic

Magnificent castle; easy Lôn Las Menai path to marina café

Walk 4

LLANRWST AND TREFRIW

Distance
4.5 miles/7.2km

Time
2¼ hours

Start/Finish
Llanrwst

Parking LL26 0LS
Watling Street car park

Cafés/pubs
Llanrwst; Trefriw

Lush meadow wildlife, peaceful riverside and elegant old spa

Walk 5

RHYD DDU TO BEDDGELERT

Distance
4.7 miles/7.6km

Time
2½ hours

Start Rhyd Ddu Station
Finish Beddgelert

Parking LL54 6TN
Rhyd Ddu Station car
park

Cafés/pubs
Rhyd Ddu; Beddgelert

Fabulous forest
and lake, Snowdon
views on good
Lôn Gwyrfai trail

Page 42

Walk 6

CWM PENAMNEN AND DOLWYDDELAN

Distance
2.1 miles/3.4km

Time
1¼ hours

Start/Finish
Dolwyddelan Station

Parking LL25 0TX
Dolwyddelan Station
car park

Cafés/pubs
Dolwyddelan

Peaceful forested
valley and Roman
road in former
bandit country

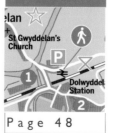

Page 48

Walk 7

LLYN MAIR

Distance
1.9 miles/3.1km

Time
1 hour

Start/Finish
Llyn Mair

Parking LL41 3AQ
Llyn Mair car park

Cafés/pubs
Tan-y-bwlch Station;
The Oakeley Arms

Idyllic lakeside
picnic; tootling
steam trains; Vale
of Ffestiniog views

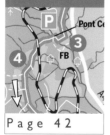

Page 54

Walk 8	Walk 9	Walk 10

GETTING OUTSIDE IN SNOWDONIA

"

Llyn Mair, an idyllic spot for a pre- or post-walk picnic

OS Champion
Lisa Wells

Llyn Mair

A very warm welcome to the new Short Walks Made Easy guide to Snowdonia – what a fantastic selection of leisurely walks we have for you!

Snowdonia, *Eryri* in Welsh, is the largest national park in Wales: covering an area of 823 square miles in the north-west quarter of the country, it is a land of legends and of spectacular natural beauty. According to Welsh mythology, Cadir Idris (seen from the Mawddach Trail between Dolgellau and Penmaenpool) was the hunting ground of the Lord of the Celtic Underworld. Discover more of this intriguing tale on walk 9.

Easy-going routes are ranged throughout the national park, from Conwy, the finest walled medieval town in Wales (if not the whole of Britain), to Victorian Barmouth, with its expansive sands and grand coastal promenade. In between, there are extensive views to Snowdon itself, the highest summit in England and Wales, and an opportunity to ride on the Welsh Highland Railway from Rhyd Ddu; the forested valley of Cwm Penamnen with romantically set Dolwyddelan Castle, location of the Disney film *Dragonslayer;* and Llyn Mair, an idyllic spot for a pre- or post-walk picnic.

In addition, there are opportunities to get outside on the coastal fringe just beyond the national park, visiting Caernarfon and its mightily imposing castle; enjoying a short circuit around the summit of the Great Orme with far-reaching panoramas to Anglesey, along the Conwy coastline, and deep into the mountains of Snowdonia; and following a secret way into Porthmadog from the tranquil haven of Borth-y-Gest.

Lisa Wells, OS Champion

WE SMILE MORE WHEN WE'RE OUTSIDE

LLyn y Gader

Whether it's a short walk during our lunch break or a full day's outdoor adventure, we know that a good dose of fresh air is just the tonic we all need.

At Ordnance Survey (OS), we're passionate about helping more people to get outside more often. It sits at the heart of everything we do, and through our products and services, we aim to help you lead an active outdoor lifestyle, so that you can live longer, stay younger and enjoy life more.

We firmly believe the outdoors is for everyone, and we want to help you find the very best Great Britain has to offer. We are blessed with an island that is beautiful and unique, with a rich and varied landscape. There are coastal paths to meander along, woodlands to explore, countryside to roam, and cities to uncover. Our trusted source of inspirational content is bursting with ideas for places to go, things to do and easy beginner's guides on how to get started.

It can be daunting when you're new to something, so we want to bring you the know-how from the people who live and breathe the outdoors. To help guide us, our team of awe-inspiring OS Champions share their favourite places to visit, hints and tips for outdoor adventures, as well as tried and tested accessible, family and wheelchair-friendly routes. We hope that you will feel inspired to spend more time outside and reap the physical and mental health benefits that the outdoors has to offer. With our handy guides, paper and digital mapping, and exciting new apps, we can be with you every step of the way.

To find out more visit os.uk/getoutside

RESPECTING
THE COUNTRYSIDE

You can't beat getting outside in the British countryside, but it's vital that we leave no trace when we're enjoying the great outdoors.

Let's make sure that generations to come can enjoy the countryside just as we do.

 Leave no trace

 Keep dogs under control; bin and bag waste

 Do not light fires; only BBQ at official sites

 Leave gates as you find them

 Keep to footpaths and open access land

 Plan ahead for your trip

For more details please visit
www.gov.uk/countryside-code

USING THIS GUIDE

Easy-to-follow Snowdonia walks for all

Before setting off
Check the walk information panel to plan your outing

- Consider using **Public transport** where flagged. If driving, note the satnav postcode for the car park under **Parking**

- The suggested **Time** is based on a gentle pace

- Note the availability of **Cafés**, tearooms and pubs, and **Toilets**

Terrain and hilliness

- **Terrain** indicates the nature of the route surface

- Any rises and falls are noted under **Hilliness**

Walking with your dog?

- This panel states where **Dogs** must be on a lead and how many stiles there are – in case you need to lift your dog

- Keep dogs on leads where there are livestock and between April and August in forest and on moorland where there are ground-nesting birds

A perfectly pocket-sized walking guide

- Handily sized for ease of use on each walk

- When not being read, it fits nicely into a pocket...

- ...so between points, put this book in the pocket of your coat, trousers or day sack and enjoy your stroll in glorious national park countryside – we've made it pocket-sized for a reason!

Flexibility of route presentation to suit all readers

- **Not comfortable map reading?** Then use the simple-to-follow route profile and accompanying route description and pictures

- **Happy to map read?** New-look walk mapping makes it easier for you to focus on the route and the points of interest along the way

- Read the insightful **Did you know?**, **Local legend**, **Stories behind the walk** and **Nature notes** to help you make the most of your day out and to enjoy all that each walk has to offer

The easy-to-use walk map

- **Large-scale** mapping for ultra-clear route finding

- **Numbered points** at key turns along the route that tie in with the route instructions and respective points marked on the profile

- **Pictorial symbols** for intuitive map reading, see Map Symbols on the front cover flap

The simple-to-follow walk profile

- Progress easily along the route using the illustrative profile, it has **numbered points** for key turning points and **graduated distance** markers

- Easy-read **route directions** with turn-by-turn detail

- Reassuring **route photographs** for each numbered point

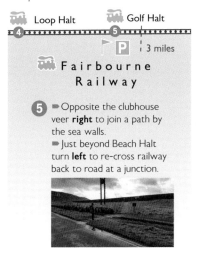

Many of the features and symbols shown are taken from Ordnance Survey's celebrated **Explorer** mapping, designed to help people across Great Britain enjoy leisure time spent outside. For more on this – and how you can start planning your own walks and adventures, please see the inside back cover.

THE GREAT ORME

The Great Orme, whose name is derived from the Norse 'urm' (sea serpent), is a gigantic tiered limestone promontory on the east side of Conwy Bay. You can get to the summit by car, via Victorian tramcars, or by chairlift from Llandudno. Incredible views are the great reward, over the town and the Little Orme – and across Conwy, its castle and bridges, the great Carneddau Mountains and the Isle of Anglesey. The grasslands are bedecked with wildflowers in spring and summer.

Distance	3 miles/4.9km
Time	1½ hours
Start/Finish	The Summit Complex, Great Orme
Parking LL30 2XF	Summit car park
Public toilets	Summit car park
Cafés/pubs	The Captain's Table café and Randolph Turpin Bar at The Summit Complex; snack bar at Summit tramway station
Terrain	Firm grass paths; stony track; tarred lanes
Hilliness	Gently undulating
Footwear	Year round

Public transport

Regular bus service, tramway and cable car link Llandudno to the Summit Complex:
www.traveline.cymru;
greatormetramway.
co.uk;
www.llandudno.com

Accessibility
....

Robust wheelchairs and all-terrain pushchair friendly route; some gradients may tax self-propelled chairs

Dogs

Welcome but keep on leads. No stiles

Did you know? Lewis Carroll was inspired to write his *Alice's Adventures in Wonderland* after a visit to Llandudno and seeing the caves, rabbit warrens and captivating scenery of the quieter corners. You can see some of the sculptures of his characters around Llandudno town centre.

Local legend St Tudno was said to have a magic whetstone. It would sharpen the swords of heroes but, if a man were a villain or coward, his sword would be blunted forever.

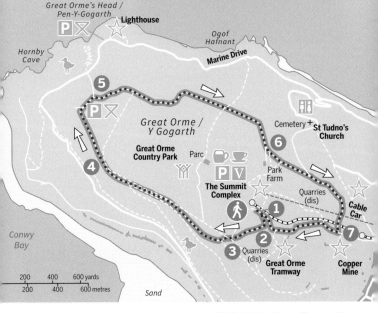

Great Orme's Head / Pen-Y-Gogarth

Lighthouse

Ogof Hafnant

Marine Drive

Hornby Cave

5

P

Great Orme / Y Gogarth

Great Orme Country Park

Parc

Cemetery + **St Tudno's Church**

6

4

The Summit Complex

P V

Park Farm

Quarries (dis)

1

Cable Car

Conwy Bay

2

3 Quarries (dis)

Great Orme Tramway

7

Copper Mine

| 200 | 400 | 600 yards |
| 200 | 400 | 600 metres |

Sand

STORIES BEHIND THE WALK

☆ **The Summit Complex** This big white house with a tower and verandas started out in 1840 as a telegraph station to relay the imminent arrival of ships with valuable cargo to Liverpool docks. In 1903 it was rebuilt as a 30-room hotel with an 18-hole golf course. The RAF used it as a radar station during World War II, and then champion middleweight boxer Randolph Turpin became a licensee of the re-opened hotel. He fell on hard times and in 1966 committed suicide.

☆ **Great Orme Tramway** The Great Orme Tramway is a cable-hauled 3 foot 6 inch-gauge track in two sections necessitating a tram change at Halfway House. The lower section opened in July 1902 and the upper a year later. It is Great Britain's sole remaining street tramway and runs from March to October.

☆The Summit Complex

Great Orme
Country Park

½ mile

▶ From car park entrance walk back down the road to footpath fingerpost.

1 ▶ Fork **right** on grass path heading towards the crags of an old quarry.

☆ Copper Mines

There have been copper mines on the Great Orme since the Bronze Age, some 4,000 years ago. They were so productive that, by 1600BC, they produced more copper than all the other mines in Britain. However, by 1400BC most of the easily accessible copper ore had been exhausted. The mines were abandoned until the 17th century when demand for copper surged, but by the 1850s all mining had again ceased. In 1987 archaeologists' excavations found the prehistoric tunnels. Today the mines are open to the public with tours available (not wheelchair accessible).

✝ St Tudno's Church

Sixth-century Christian missionary, Tudno, who gave his name to Llandudno, built a church on the Great Orme. It is believed that he was one of seven sons born to King Seithenyn whose kingdom in Cardigan Bay was submerged by the rising tides. The building you see today dates back to the 12th century with 15th-century additions.

4	5	
1 mile	P ✕	1½ miles

2 ➡ Take next fork **right**, the path angling right beneath the quarry.
➡ Descend to wall corner on the **right**.

3 ➡ Choose either path: the smoother one follows the wall; the slightly rougher path hugs the edge, giving even better views.
➡ They merge near the next wall corner.

NATURE NOTES

The Great Orme is a Site of Special Scientific Interest, designated for its diverse vegetation, ranging from marine grassland to acid heath. On the marine grasslands many of the well-known limestone species are present – wild thyme, bloody cranesbill, both common and hoary variety of rock roses, and the pretty sky-blue spring squill.

The cliffs are colonised by many gulls, including fulmars, kittiwakes, guillemots and razorbills.

On the heathland you can see both ling, the most commonly seen moorland heather, and bell heather, which has a brighter larger flower. Scattered among it you will see dwarf and common gorse, and in places the pungent-smelling juniper, which will remind you of a gin and tonic.

If you see a group of noisy little birds they will probably be linnets. This chestnut coloured finch nests here in great numbers.

Juniper

6

i 2 miles

4 ➡ As the wall bends right by an ancient cairn, keep **ahead** towards a marker post and car park.
➡ At car park turn **right** along rough concrete road to the first left bend.

5 ➡ At bend, take path on **right** (slightly rough initially).
➡ This climbs gently back to the wall.
➡ Follow wall to the drive to Park Farm (Y Parc).

Razorbill

Bell heather

Linnet

Sky-blue spring squill

St Tudno's Church   Great Orme   Copper   The Summit
(450 yards)   ☆ Tramway   ☆ Mines   ☆ Complex

2½ miles   3 miles

6 ➤ Fork **left** on main stony track to a road by a lay-by car park.

➤ Bear **right** onto road; follow it to cross the tramway (note Halfway Station to left).

➤ Keep **forward** to T-junction.

7 ➤ Turn **right**, soon passing copper mine, back uphill to the Summit car park (note for much of the way there are grass paths along the roadside).

AROUND CONWY

Conwy, the finest small medieval town in Wales, has an exquisite position on the Conwy Estuary, its castle and tall town walls towering over cottages, inns, cafés and shops. The quayside echoes to the sound of gulls and you may see fishermen untangling their nets and emptying their mussel baskets. Starting from the modern marina, this fine route discovers the town, its castle, ancient buildings and bridges and the wooded knoll of Bodlondeb. There's also a stroll along the beach with views to the Great Orme.

Distance	3.8 miles/6.1km
Time	2 hours
Start/Finish	Conwy Marina
Parking LL32 8GJ	Beacons car park, Beacons Way, Conwy Marina
Public toilets	Conwy Quay
Cafés/pubs	Conwy Marina, quayside and in Conwy
Terrain	Pavement, tarred paths; stony track and sandy beach path
Hilliness	Mostly flat, one climb from quayside to castle

Did you know? Aberconwy Abbey was founded by Cistercian monks from Strata Florida in Mid Wales and patronised by Llywelyn the Great. Most of the buildings have been destroyed but parts of the abbey remain in the walls of the Church of St Mary and All Saints, which stands in the heart of the town.

Local legend Long ago local fishermen caught a mermaid. Despite her pleas to be set free, they paraded their catch around Conwy. With her last gasping breath the mermaid cursed the town. Ghostly laughter was heard when the town hall, which was built on the spot she had died, burned to the ground.

Footwear
Year round

Public transport
Bus and train services to Conwy, www.traveline.cymru

Accessibility
Wheelchair and pushchair friendly, except the beach path beyond **8** (see alternative route)

Dogs
Welcome but keep on leads. No stiles

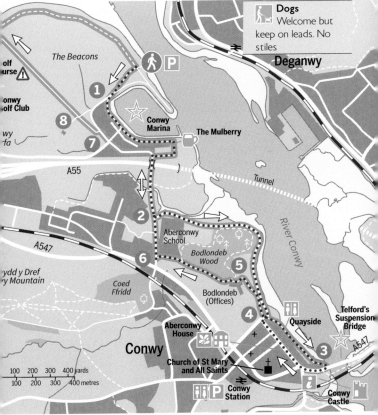

STORIES BEHIND THE WALK

☆**Conwy Marina** In 1986 Conwy Morfa (beach) was converted into a dry dock for the building of the A55 road tunnel under the Afon (river) Conwy. On completion the dry dock was converted into what is now Conwy Marina. The Mulberry pub was named in commemoration of the Mulberry Harbour Phoenix Caissons that were built on the Morfa to help with the Normandy Landings of World War II.

🏰 **Conwy Castle**
Conwy's castle belongs to a fairytale. It dates back to 1287 when English King Edward I built it as part of his 'iron ring' to repress the rebellious troops of Llywelyn the Great, who had staunchly resisted his conquest of Wales. A statue of the revered Welsh prince can be seen in Lancaster Square.

Conwy Marina ☆   The Mulberry ☕   ¹ ½ mile

1 ➤ Turn **left** to follow block pavement round the marina.
➤ Turn **right** beyond The Mulberry (pub). Cross the complex and car park out to road.
➤ Turn **right** along road, then **left** to cross a bridge over the A55. Keep **forward** to school.

2 Aberconwy School   Bodlon Wo

2 ➤ At Aberconwy School turn **left**; follow tarred path which soon rounds Bodlondeb Wood to the quayside.
➤ Follow promenade; nearing the castle and bridges, rise to main road.

➤ From car park go back along the lane towards the marina.
➤ Walk to first house on the left.

☆ **Telford's Suspension Bridge** Three fine bridges cross the estuary to the town walls of this medieval World Heritage Site. The most aesthetically pleasing one is Thomas Telford's magnificent suspension bridge of 1822, which was built to carry the London to Holyhead road across the Conwy Estuary. Like the bridge itself, the toll collector's lodge was built to blend in with the Norman architecture of the castle.

☆ **Historic Conwy** Within the 6 foot-thick and 35 foot-high town walls there are some notable ancient buildings. The half-timbered Aberconwy House has its origins in the 14th century, although most of the structure dates to around 1500. This old merchant's house is now owned by the National Trust. The equally impressive Plas Mawr is a large, restored mansion, built for the Wynn family of Gwydir Castle in 1576.

Telford's Suspension Bridge ☆   Conwy Castle   Aberconwy House ④

Quayside   ③

'1 mile   '1½ miles

③ ➤ Turn **right** beneath castle ramparts to a roundabout; follow the pavement on the right as it curves into Castle Street.
➤ Go **ahead** on Castle Street to crossroads by the Manor House.
➤ Keep **forward** into Berry Street to an arch in town walls.

④ ➤ Through archway, as the road bends left uphill, go **straight on** (no entry sign) along the driveway to Bodlondeb offices.
➤ Keep on main drive to reach footpath just beyond the impressive Conwy Council building.

NATURE NOTES

Among the marram grass of the Morfa Conwy shoreline you might see a scattering of yellow horned poppy, the tiny blue flowers of sea holly or the pink and white sea bindweed. These attract many pollinating insects, including painted lady, common blue and meadow brown butterflies. And then there's the extremely rare and protected belted beauty moth.

Bodlondeb Wood cloaks a knoll of volcanic rock lying between the town harbour and the beach. The wood has many tree varieties, both conifer and broadleaved. These include Scots pine, beech, sessile oak, hornbeam and cedars. You'll almost certainly see grey squirrels in the woods and possibly sparrowhawks, one of the smaller birds of prey. Nuthatches and jays are occasionally seen here too.

Nuthatch

5   2 miles   Council Offices   Bodlondeb Wood   6   Morfa Drive   Aberconwy School   2½ miles   Ellis Way   7

6 ► Turn **right** along road (Morfa Drive) back to **2** by the school.
► Go straight on, retracing earlier steps to cross bridge over A55.
► To avoid sandy path/beach, wheelchairs/pushchairs should continue to retrace steps to car park; otherwise turn **left** along Ellis Way to a roundabout.

5 ► Take shortcut path on **left** behind the offices.
► Resume along drive to reach car park and turn **right** along a tarred track.
► Walk this for 450 yards to a T-junction shortly beyond a zebra crossing.

Sea holly

Pink sea bindweed

Jay

Yellow horned poppy

Golf Club

3 miles ⚠️   Morfa Conwy   3½ miles   The Beacons

7 ➡ Go **straight on** at roundabout.
➡ In 200 yards, as road bends right, turn **left** through gate and keep forward on golf course track to an intersection.

8 ➡ Turn **right** heading for the beach. At the shore go **right**. A sandy, sometimes stony path then follows the coast.
➡ As you approach a jetty, fork **right** to arrive back at car park.

Walk 2 Around Conwy **25**

This page (clockwise): salt marshes, Mawddach Estuary; Glaslyn Estuary with the Moelwyn mountains; Conwy Castle; Y Garn, Ryd Dhu. Opposite (clockwise): Barmouth ferry station; Great Orme; Ynysgyffylog.

26

CAERNARFON TO PORT DINORWIC

Coastal Caernarfon with its fine Norman castle and town walls, its quaint narrow streets and maritime history, offers a spectacular start to this easy-paced walk. The route follows Lôn Las Menai on the course of an old railway linking Bangor and Caernarfon. Surfaced in its entirety, it offers fine views of the Menai Strait before passing through avenues of broadleaved trees. Always there's the sound of seabirds and surf echoing through the breeze en route to picturesque Port Dinorwic and its waterside cafés.

Distance	4 miles/6.5km
Time	2 hours
Start Caernarfon	
Finish Port Dinorwic	
Parking LL55 1TH	Shell Site car park, Balaclava Road
Public toilets	Corner of Balaclava Road and Crown Street, Caernarfon; Y Felinheli, opposite the Garddfon Inn ⑤
Cafés/pubs	Caernarfon; Garddfon Inn, Y Felinheli; The Swellies (café) and Hen Lechan (bar), Port Dinorwic
Terrain	Tarred track, pavement and lanes
Hilliness	One descent to seafront in Y Felinheli; one ascent from Port Dinorwic to bus stop

Footwear
Year round

 Public transport
Frequent bus service between Y Felinheli and Caernarfon, www.arrivabus.co.uk/wales

Accessibility
▥▥▥▥▥▥▥▥▥▥
Wheelchair and pushchair friendly; the climb from Port Dinorwic to bus stop may not be suitable for manual wheelchairs

Dogs
Welcome but keep on leads – shared-use path with cyclists. No stiles

Did you know? The Romans, under Gnaeus Julius Agricola, conquered the local Ordovices tribe and built their fort, Segontium, in AD77 in the heart of Caernarfon. It would have had defences of earth and timber, with gates and parallel streets. At the height of its powers it would have housed 1,000 troops. Coins discovered on archaeological digs show that the Romans occupied Segontium until about AD394.

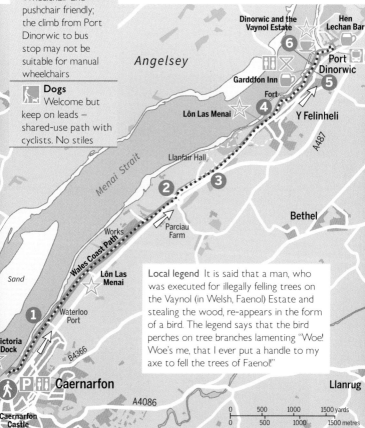

Local legend It is said that a man, who was executed for illegally felling trees on the Vaynol (in Welsh, Faenol) Estate and stealing the wood, re-appears in the form of a bird. The legend says that the bird perches on tree branches lamenting "Woe! Woe's me, that I ever put a handle to my axe to fell the trees of Faenol!"

STORIES BEHIND THE WALK

Caernarfon Castle This most imposing of Edward I's 13th-century 'iron ring' castles was built to subdue the troublesome Welsh and their warring princes. Erected on the site of a Norman motte and bailey castle, its huge stone polygonal towers and tall ramparts are remarkably intact for its age. In 1969 it was the setting for Prince Charles' investiture, some 700 years after Edward made his son the first English Prince of Wales here. The castle, now under the care of CADW, also houses the regimental Museum of the Royal Welch Fusiliers.

☆ **Lôn Las Menai** This long-distance cycle and walkway is built on the line of the Bangor to Caernarfon railway. When the railway was first built it had its Caernarfon terminus where the supermarket is now (near the start) – the line was later extended by way of a tunnel to the town centre. Earmarked for closure under the Beeching cuts, the railway lasted until 1972 as it was needed to bring in guests to Caernarfon at Prince Charles' investiture as Prince of Wales in 1969.

Caernarfon
Castle (½ mile)

½ mile

Lôn Las
Menai ☆

☆ Victoria Dock
(600 yards)

Menai
Strait

Waterloo
Port

1 m

- The route, highlighted by blue Lôn Las Menai signs, begins on the coast side of the car park.
- Turn **right** along the tarred track for almost ½ mile to meet a crossing residential road at Waterloo Port.

1
- Take the ongoing narrower parallel path, **ahead-right**.
- This rejoins old railway trackbed beyond the houses.
- Continue on Lôn Las Menai for 1½ miles to large roundabout.

☆ Dinorwic and the Vaynol Estate

Y Felinheli, translated as the mill by the (river) Heulyn, was part of the Vaynol Estate, owned by the powerful Assheton Smith family, who also owned the Dinorwic Quarry near Llanberis. The family built the docks at Port Dinorwic in 1793 and the Dinorwic narrow-gauge railway (1848) between quarry and port. Slate was shipped around the world from here. The last quarry-owned steamer ceased operations in 1955.

☆ Victoria Dock

Situated near the start of the walk, Victoria Dock was completed in 1874, principally for importing Scandinavian timber but it also dealt in general trade for the town. The North East Coast Aircraft Company relocated here during World War II and trained workers to make parts for many famous RAF planes. Later in the war they were employed to make engine casings for the Gloster Meteor. Today the dock is a dedicated yacht marina.

1½ miles   2 miles

2 ➧ At roundabout take the tarred cycleway alongside the second exit **left**, signed Y Felinheli.
➧ Continue beside road for ⅓ mile to a fork.

3 ➧ Here track bears **left** away from road.
➧ Walk on for another ¾ mile to junction with road by Y Felinheli Health Centre (left).

NATURE NOTES

Formed over 20,000 years ago, gouged by glaciers flowing down from the mountains of Snowdonia, the Menai Strait is a major geological fault dividing the Isle of Anglesey from mainland Wales. It's a haven for wading birds, many of whom use the area as a stop-off on their spring and autumn migrations. The sandbanks are important feeding grounds for waders and you may well spot little egret, oystercatcher, redshank and curlew.

Rather than rounding Anglesey, many seals and porpoises swim along the strait on their way to Liverpool Bay.

Avenues of birch, oak and sycamore line the route. The first two are native to Britain but the sycamore, part of the acer family, was introduced from Europe in the Middle Ages. Some believe it could have been imported by the Romans.

Common ivy climbs up the tree trunks and boughs, offering much-needed colour to the landscape in the winter months, while many ferns, including hart's tongue, proliferate beneath.

Winter heliotrope adds a touch of colour in the early months of the year. This plant grows in large patches of heart-shaped leaves.

Wales Coastal Path

② Roundabout

③ Y Felinheli | 2½ miles
Health Centre

3 miles

④ ➧ Turn **left** down Beach Road to Y Felinheli.
➧ Pass boatyards, a couple of warehouses and a playground to reach Garddfon Inn.

⑤ ➧ Beyond the inn follow the lane **right** but then immediately go **left** along a waymarked ginnel past houses.
➧ The narrow alley soon meets a road (Hen Gei Llechi).

Above: redshank **Below**: oystercatcher

Top: winter heliotrope
Above: common ivy

Lôn Las Menai

Beach Road

Garddfon Inn

Port Dinorwic

Dinorwic and the Vaynol Estate

3½ miles

Hen Gei Llechi

4 miles

6 ➡ Keep **ahead** on residential road, rounding **right-hand** bend to Port Dinorwic Marina.
➡ For the bus back to Caernarfon, continue beyond Hen Lechan Bar up lane to main road (Bangor Street). Turn **right** and bus stop is 150 yards on left.

Curlew

GO BY TRAIN
CATCH A BUS

LLANRWST AND TREFRIW

The River Conwy begins life as Llyn Conwy, a sombre lake set high in Snowdonia's moorland wilderness to the south. By the time it reaches Llanrwst it is mature and meanders among emerald floodplains flanked by forest-clad hills. This gentle walk discovers the Cob, grassy ramparts built to protect the area from major flooding. You'll visit the spa village of Trefriw, and see two fine bridges over the Conwy: the Gower Suspension Bridge and Pont Fawr, a graceful thee-arched stone bridge.

Distance	4.5 miles / 7.2 km
Time	2¼ hours
Start/Finish	Llanrwst
Parking LL26 0LS	Watling Street car park
Public toilets	Llanrwst; Trefriw at ❹
Cafés/pubs	Llanrwst; Trefriw
Terrain	Pavement; lane; farm track; grassy embankment
Hilliness	Mostly flat
Footwear	Winter 🥾 Spring/Summer/ Autumn 👟

Did you know? The Romans built their Sarn Helen road through Trefriw, linking forts at Caerhun near Conwy to Tomen-y-mur near Trawsfynydd before continuing to settlements in South Wales.

Local legend It is said that occasionally the ghost of a lady, usually dressed in white or grey, appears in the North Wing of Gwydir Castle near Llanrwst, the home of the Wynn family. It has been said she is the ghost of a young maid seduced by the infamous and cruel Sir John Wynn. When the baronet tired of her he had her murdered and walled up in the castle. She's known as the Lady of Gwydir Castle.

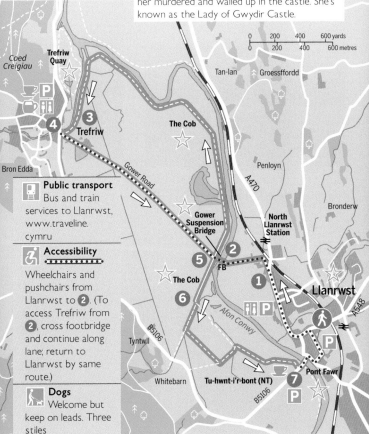

Public transport
Bus and train services to Llanrwst, www.traveline. cymru

Accessibility
Wheelchairs and pushchairs from Llanrwst to ②. (To access Trefriw from ②, cross footbridge and continue along lane; return to Llanrwst by same route.)

Dogs
Welcome but keep on leads. Three stiles

STORIES BEHIND THE WALK

☆ **Llanrwst** When King Edward I decreed that no Welsh man should work within ten miles of his newly built Conwy Castle it gave a boost to Llanrwst, which at 13 miles away was the nearest settlement. The small town grew largely from the wool trade and its position as the lowest bridging point (in those times) of the Conwy. The stone coffin of Edward's arch enemy Llywelyn the Great can be seen in the parish church of St Grwst.

☆ **Pont Fawr**
The three-arched bridge in Llanrwst, known as Pont Fawr, was designed by the famous 17th-century architect Inigo Jones. By its side is Tu-hwnt-i'r-bont, a pretty 15th-century house owned by the National Trust and used as a café.

Gower Suspension Bridge

Gower Suspension ☆ Bridge

☆ Llanrwst — North Llanrwst ⇌ Station — ½ mile — River Conwy — 1 mile

➤ Leave car park entrance/exit and turn **right** along Watling Street.
➤ Go **left** at the end.
➤ Keep **ahead** past the end of the square and bend **right** on Station Road. Continue for 450 yards to zebra crossing.

1 ➤ Just beyond crossing, take shallow fork on **left** (continuation of Station Road).
➤ As it reaches North Llanrwst Station, turn **left** along lane (Gower Road).
➤ Walk to suspension bridge and cross river.

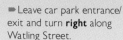

☆ **Trefriw Quay** The Conwy was navigable all the way from the estuary to Trefriw, whose quay was visited by regular passenger boats, including paddle steamers, until 1939. A journey from Conwy town took 90 minutes. The quay was developed by the Wynn family of nearby Gwydir Castle and dredging allowed boats of up to 100 tons to reach it. Grain, wool, hide, timber and lead from the Gwydir Forest mines were shipped out from here. Today, the remains of the quay are visible but are overgrown and silted up.

The Spa

The spa waters of Trefriw Wells, which are rich in iron and sulphur, were known to have been used by the Romans, who first discovered the mineral water caves. There were further minor developments in the 1700s, but in 1863 Lord Willoughby built a small bathhouse, and then the much larger current building. Today, the Spa mineral waters of the village are bottled and sent around the world.

Trefriw Woollen Mill

☆
¦ The Cob

1½ miles ¦

2 miles ¦

2 ▪ Turn **right** over stile and continue along grassy flood bank (the Cob), river on right, for 1½ miles, passing through 8 kissing-gates.

3 ▪ Through last gate, keep **forward** on farm track on outskirts of Trefriw.
▪ Then take narrow enclosed track on **right** to emerge by public toilets set back from the main road.

NATURE NOTES

Kingfishers have been spotted on the Conwy at Llanrwst. These small, bright orange and blue birds love still, tree-lined water and are, as their name suggests, expert at catching fish – they move at lightning speed when their prey is sighted.

Herons can also be seen wading or standing stock still, waiting for a catch.

Top: kingfisher
Above: sheep on the Cob
Left: heron

☆ Trefriw Quay

3

Trefriw ¦ 2½ miles

4

Gower Road

¦ 3 miles

Gower Suspension Bridge ☆

5

River Conwy

4 ➥ Turn right on main road for facilities in Trefriw.
➥ Route continues **left** along lane (Gower Road). Follow it back to the suspension bridge. (Note: for part of the way there is a well-surfaced, tree-lined path on the left.)

5 ➥ Before bridge, turn **right** over stile and follow the Cob for 350 yards to next stile.

The Cob

Both Trefriw and Llanrwst lie on the Conwy's floodplain. It's a part of nature that it floods. However, that's no good for the villages in harm's way and there is a need to form defences. In 2004, Trefriw was cut off by floods for three days with up to three feet of water on High Street. And so they built the Cob, where raised embankments hold the waters back. The current flood defence additions were made in 2010, at a cost of £7m.

Above: common blue
Below: red admiral

The Cob   Tu-hwnt-i'r-bont (NT) ☕   Pont Fawr ☆   Llanrwst 4½ miles ☆

3½ miles   4 miles   River Conwy 🅿

6 ► Go **left** over stile to leave the Cob and follow narrow path along the left side of it.
► This joins farm track at a corner. Turn **left** along it, later to follow it round two bends, continuing to road T-junction.

7 ► Turn **left** to pass National Trust tea rooms. Cross bridge back into Llanrwst and turn **right**.
► Then turn first **left** along Conwy Terrace. Beyond next bend this becomes Watling Street; car park is up on the **right**.

Walk 4 Llanrwst and Trefriw 39

Opposite (clockwise):
short-eared owl; ringlet on
bramble; foxglove.
This page (clockwise):
Great Orme goat; pine marten;
larch cones

40

RHYD DDU TO BEDDGELERT

This route follows the Lôn Gwyrfai trail as it forges a way over the Ffridd Uchaf blanket bog, round the beautiful Llyn y Gader and through Beddgelert Forest. The path is always well surfaced with fine views of Snowdon and the rocky escarpment of Y Garn. The Welsh Highland Railway is encountered several times before reaching Beddgelert and there is a halt at Meillionen Station if you need to get back to Rhyd Ddu early. Beddgelert is a must to explore with its tea shops, inns and the lovely Glaslyn river.

Distance	4.7 miles/7.6km
Time	2½ hours
Start Rhyd Ddu station	
Finish Beddgelert Station	
Parking	LL54 6TN Rhyd Ddu Station car park
Public toilets	Rhyd Ddu Station car park; Beddgelert Station (when open); Stryd Smith, Beddgelert
Cafés/pubs	Rhyd Ddu and Beddgelert
Terrain	Gravel-surfaced track; lane
Hilliness	Gentle inclines in Beddgelert Forest
Footwear	Year round

Did you know? Beddgelert and surrounding area have made it to Hollywood: many scenes from Ingrid Bergman's film *Inn of the Sixth Happiness* were shot here, as were some scenes from *Tomb Raider 2*, starring Angelina Jolie.

Local legend Llywelyn the Great left his baby boy in the care of his dog, Gelert. On his return he found the child's cot empty, and when the bloodstained Gelert came to greet him he feared the worst and ran his sword through the hound. But then Llywelyn heard the cries of his unharmed child, and next to him the body of a huge wolf, killed by the dutiful Gelert.

Public transport
Regular bus service between Beddgelert and Rhyd Ddu, www.traveline/cymru. Welsh Highland Railway, www.whr.co.uk

Accessibility
Wheelchairs to the far side of Llyn y Gadar; pushchairs throughout

Dogs
Welcome but keep on leads. No stiles

| 0 | 500 | 1000 yards |
| 0 | 500 | 1000 metres |

Map labels:
B4418
Afon
Rhyd Ddu Station
FB
1
Llyn y Gader
Welsh Highland Railway
Lôn Gwyrfai
Cwm-du
Beddgelert Forest
2
P
Pont Ceffylau
3
FB
Llyn Llywelyn
4
A4085
5
6
Meillionen Station
Lôn Gwyrfai
Welsh Highland Railway
Beddgelert Forest
7
Ford
A498
Afon Glaslyn
Beddgelert Station
Beddgelert
Church of St Mary
Ford
8
Cwm Gloch Farm
Gelert's Grave
Afon Glochig

STORIES BEHIND THE WALK

☆ **Beddgelert Forest**

 Welsh Highland Railway The original Welsh Highland Railway started out in 1921 but was not a success. It stumbled along until it was closed in 1933. The Welsh Highland Railway Society took steps to restore it in the 1960s and opened up short stretches in Porthmadog and Caernarfon. After much wrangling it was taken over by the Ffestiniog Railway in the 1990s and stage by stage was opened all the way from Caernarfon to Porthmadog.

The 1,730-acre forest beneath the Moel Hebog mountain range is mainly planted with conifers such as Norway and Sitka spruce and larch, together with broadleaved species like birch and oak. It's a working forest but has many leisure facilities: a campsite, lodges, the steam railway, and walking and cycling trails. Pont Ceffylau, which you'll cross halfway along the walk, is Grade II listed and carried the pre-turnpike road over the Afon (river) Hafod-Ruffydd-Isaf. It was damaged by floods but was rebuilt in 1844.

Rhyd Ddu Station

Llyn y Gader   ½ mile   **Beddgelert Forest** ☆

Footbridge ☆ **L ô n G w y r f a i   t r a i l** 1 mile

1 ▰ Over bridge, continue across gated causeway, rounding Llyn y Gader to a disused quarry.
▰ The track then rises to enter Beddgelert Forest through a gate.
▰ Stay with trail to fingerposted T-junction in ½ mile.

▰ From the car park, cross road and go through ornate gate opposite.
▰ Follow surfaced path to footbridge.

☆ Beddgelert

Beddgelert, which means Gelert's grave, takes its name from the Celtic saint, Celert. The pretty village lies tucked away near the confluence of the Glaslyn and Colwyn rivers, beneath the lusciously wooded lower crags and bluffs of Snowdon. In the heart of the village is a pretty twin-arched stone bridge over the chattering Glaslyn. Nearby is the spectacular Aberglaslyn Gorge, where sheer cliffs tower above the now roaring white waters of the Glaslyn and the little trains of the Welsh Highland Railway.

+ Church of St Mary

St Mary's, whose west walls were built in the 12th century, has origins going back even further, to the Celtic saints of the 6th century. An Augustinian priory was established in the 13th century and gained influence through the support of Welsh noblemen, including Llywelyn the Great.

Gelert's Grave

1½ miles ❷ ┊ 2 miles ❸

☆ Lôn Gwyrfai trail P

❷ ▪ Turn **left**, signed 'Beddgelert', and descend to cross Welsh Highland Railway (WHR).

▪ Turn **right** along forest road parallel to railway.

▪ Keep **straight on** at next junction; pass car park and continue to next junction beyond a house.

❸ ▪ Go **right** and soon cross stone bridge (Pont Ceffylau).

▪ Keep **ahead** crossing WHR. The forest road bends **left** then rises gradually to a farm drive junction.

NATURE NOTES

Goosander is a year-round visitor to Llyn y Gader, while the common sandpiper can be seen in spring and summer. In winter you may be able to see the whooper swan. Frogs and water voles also thrive here.

The Gwyrfai, which outflows from Llyn y Gader, has been designated a Special Area of Conservation due to its biodiversity. Otters, salmon, Arctic char and floating water plantain can be found here. The lake is surrounded by the blanket bog known as Ffridd Uchaf. It's a great store for carbon and vital in the strategy to combat climate change.

Above: whooper swan
Left: goosander

Pont Ceffylau | **4** 2½ miles | **5** 3 miles | Welsh Highland Railway 🚂 | Meillionen Station **6** | 3½ mile

☆ **L ô n   G w y r f a i   t r a i l**

4 ➡ Fork **right**. Bend **left** with track at next junction.
➡ Pass a viewpoint/bench and stay **left**.
➡ Keep **left** at the following junction and descend to reach fork.

5 ➡ Leave main track here for signed gravel path on **right**.
➡ It leads to another forest road, which descends to Meillionen Station (WHR).

6 ➡ Turn **right** before level crossing, passing holiday chalets.
➡ Keep with main track parallel to railway for 350 yards then fork **right** at next junction.
➡ In another 450 yards reach junction at a hairpin bend.

Otter

Water vole

The Sitka spruce, a large, evergreen conifer, was first imported from the west coast of North America. It was popular with foresters due to its propensity for growing quickly in poor soils where it can reach 330 feet tall. Its name derives from the region of Sitka in Alaska.

☆ Beddgelert Forest

🚂 Beddgelert Station

Gelert's Grave (650 yards) ☆

⌗ Church of St Mary (400 yards)

7 ——— 4 miles ┆ Cwm Gloch Farm 8 ——— 4½ miles ┆ ☆ Beddgelert

☆ L ô n G w y r f a i t r a i l

7 ➡ Branch **left** on gravel path descending to cross a stepped footbridge.
➡ Leaving the forest, follow the path across open ground to Cwm Gloch Farm.

8 ➡ Through gate turn **left** along gravelled lane.
➡ Follow it over WHR twice before passing beneath it just before reaching Beddgelert Station. P

Walk 5 Rhyd Ddu to Beddgelert **47**

CWM PENAMNEN
& DOLWYDDELAN

Dolwyddelan is off the beaten track. The romantic keep of its 13th-century castle looks down on the village rooftops. This walk in the peaceful afforested valley of Cwm Penamnen, once terrorised by bandits, passes beneath the huge climbers' crags of Carreg Alltrem, then comes back on a Roman road, leading past the ruins of 15th-century cottages. For most of the way there's a tremendous view across the main Lledr valley to the gnarled cliffs of Moel Siabod.

Distance	2.1 miles/3.4km
Time	1¼ hours
Start/Finish	Dolwyddelan Station
Parking LL25 0TX	Station car park
Public toilets	On village main road near Y Gwydyr pub
Cafés/pubs	Dolwyddelan
Terrain	Stony forest paths; tarred lane
Hilliness	Steady climb outward; steady descent on return
Footwear	Winter 👢 Spring/Summer/Autumn 👟

Public transport
Bus and train services to Dolwyddelan from Llandudno and Blaenau Ffestiniog, www. traveline.cymru

Accessibility
Route surfaces are probably too rough for wheelchairs throughout; suitable for all-terrain pushchairs

Dogs
Welcome. No stiles

Did you know?
Dolwyddelan Castle and the surrounding countryside was used as a location for the Disney film *Dragonslayer*.

Local legend When powerful Welsh ruler Owain Gwynedd died he left 13 sons. A bloody succession dispute arose among the siblings. Two of the sons, Madoc and Rhirid were appalled by the greed and violence and wanted nothing to do with their family. They boarded a ship from Rhos-on-Sea on a voyage of discovery across the Atlantic. They found America. It is said that they married local indigenous women and for many decades there were Welsh-speaking Native Americans.

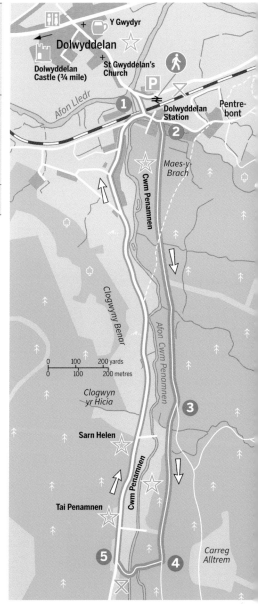

STORIES BEHIND
THE WALK

 Dolwyddelan Castle Beneath the stone walls of Dolwyddelan Castle lies a small pine copse, obscuring a grassy knoll upon which perched an older wooden castle known as Tomen Castell. The castle was probably built around 1170 by Iorwerth Drwyndwn, father of Llywelyn the Great, Prince of Wales. His descendants built the stone castle above in the 13th century and held onto it until Edward I took it from Llywelyn ap Grufydd during his march across northern Wales in 1283.

☆ **Dolwyddelan village**
The small village relied on slate quarrying in the Lledr Valley and local hills for its early growth. It was often referred to as Dolyddelen in Victorian times. Both names mean Gwyddelan's meadow, referring to Saint Gwyddelan. The village church is dedicated to her.

 Dolwyddelan Castle (¾ mile)

☕ Y Gwydyr

☆ **Dolwyddelan village** (375 yards)

🚻

✚ St Gwyddelan's Church

🚉 Dolwyddelan Station

🅿
✗

☆ **C w m   P e n a m n e n**

½ mile

🠖 Bear **left** out of car park in front of the school.
🠖 At junction turn **left** to cross over railway bridge.

1 🠖 Turn **left** along the lane signed Pentre Bont High Street, passing Rathbone Terrace to next junction.

☆ **Tai Penamnen** You'll pass the ruins of Tai Penamnen, a 15th-century cottage enlarged by Maredudd ap Ieuan, whose family later became the powerful Wynns. Unfortunately, bandits, who had settled in nearby Ysbyty Ifan, marauded the valley regularly, forcing the Wynns into the Conwy Valley, where they re-built the fortified manor of Gwydir, now Gwydir Castle. The whole region was for centuries part of the Wynn Estate.

☆ Sarn Helen
The lane used on the return route is part of Sarn Helen, a 160-mile Roman road between Conwy and Carmarthen. It was probably named after Elen of the Hosts, the wife of Emperor Magnus Maximus. On leaving Dolwyddelan it climbs out of Cwm Penamnen onto the wild moors above, passing through the slate quarries between Cwm Penmachno and Blaenau Ffestiniog before reaching the Roman fort at Tomen-y-mur, above Trawsfynydd.

Carreg Alltrem ④
1 mile

③

☆ C w m   P e n a m n e n

② ➡ Turn **right** at next junction (blue waymark arrow).
➡ Follow stony forestry track for just over ½ mile, rising steadily though the valley's coniferous woodland to waymarked (blue and red) track junction.

③ ➡ Fork **right**, the forest road, now levelling out.
➡ Continue for ⅓ mile to next waymarked and fingerposted junction.

NATURE NOTES

In the nature reserve by the station car park there's an information panel telling you all about the wildlife and plants. Underneath the boughs of silver birch and willow is grassland rich with wildflowers such as violet, primrose, wild rose and wood anemone. If you're lucky you might see a jay, but wrens, blue tits and robins are more regular visitors. The field vole and wood mouse is also common.

Top: wren
Above: blue tit
Left: violets

☆ Tai Penamnen   ☆ Sarn Helen

⑤ Afon Cwm Penamnen

1½ miles

④ ➡ Turn **right** off forestry track on path signed Pont Carreg Alltrem.
➡ This soon crosses a footbridge over the river (Afon Penamnen) leading to small picnic site and tarred lane.

⑤ ➡ Turn **right** along lane – the Sarn Helen Roman road – to pass the ruins of Tai Penamnen.
➡ Remain on lane all the way back to railway bridge ❶.
➡ Turn **left** over railway and then **right** to the car park.

Wood anemone

Top: wood mouse
Above: field vole

Dolwyddelan
Castle (¾ mile)
Y Gwydyr

Dolwyddelan ☆
village (375 yards)

St Gwyddelan's Church ✚

Dolwyddelan Station ⇌

☆ C w m   P e n a m n e n

2 miles

Autumn in Cwm Penamnen

If you come to Cwm Penamnen outside the summer months you'll notice the contrast between the reddish colours of the European larch and the green of the Sitka spruce trees. Unusually for a conifer the larch is deciduous, which means it loses is needles in the autumn. This fine graceful tree is distinguishable in spring too for its new needles are a much brighter lime green compared to the spruce. The larch has small cones, which may stay on the tree for many years.

CATCH A STEAM TRAIN

LLYN MAIR

You could start this outing with a lakeside picnic for it's an idyllic place, or take tea at the Tan-y-bwlch Station café in the woods above the car park. Wide forest tracks take the route up through the trees with the waters of the lake glinting through their boughs. The walk crosses the narrow-gauge steam railway, so look out for trains, their plumes of smoke or listen for their toots. Enjoy, too, occasional views of the beautiful Vale of Ffestiniog.

Distance
1.9 miles/3.1km

Time
1 hour

Start/Finish
Llyn Mair

Parking LL41 3AQ
Llyn Mair car park and picnic site, Tan-y-bwlch

Public toilets
Opposite the Oakeley Arms, Tan-y-bwlch

Cafés/pubs
Seasonal cafés at Tan-y-bwlch Station and Plâs Tan-y-bwlch; The Oakeley Arms, Tan-y-bwlch; The Grapes, Maentwrog

Terrain
Forest tracks

Hilliness
Some short ascents and descents, but generally rising over the first half of the walk and descending over the second

Footwear
Winter 🥾
Spring/Summer/Autumn 👟

Did you know? From the 1890s Llyn Mair supplied the head of water that enabled a hydro-electric scheme to supply power to Plâs Tan-y-bwlch. It is believed to be the first house in North Wales with electric lighting powered from its own station.

Local legend Twrog was a 7th-century Christian giant. He was so appalled to discover pagan worship in the valley that he tossed a great stone down the hill to destroy their altar. This act gave the village its name, Maentwrog, which means Twrog's Stone. The stone is believed to be the one lying in the churchyard. It is said if anyone rubs the stone, fate will decree that they shall return to the village.

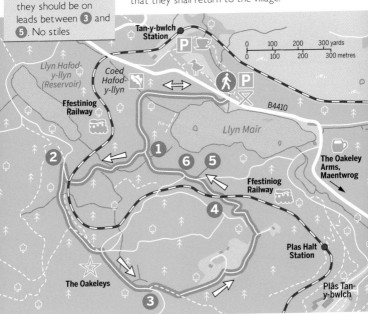

STORIES BEHIND THE WALK

☆ The Oakeleys

The walk as a whole crosses the forests of the Oakeley Estate. The influential family, who were huge benefactors to the local community, lived in Plâs Tan-y-bwlch, which lies just south of this walk. They built embankments in the valley below, which kept the tidal river at bay and improved the quality of the agricultural lands and funded many of the buildings in Maentwrog.

Oakeley memorials, St Twrog's churchyard

Coed Hafod-y-llyn

Llyn Mair and the smaller Llyn Hafod-y-llyn nestle in woodland known as Coed Hafod-y-llyn, which is managed by the Woodland Trust. Many of the paths are permissive so everyone has to look after them. The wood is part of the wider area known as Dyffryn Maentwrog. Timber from the oak trees on the estate was used to build ships in Porthmadog and as props for the slate mines. Besides being the source of a hydro-electric scheme, Llyn Mair was built by William Edward Oakeley as a birthday present for his daughter Mair (Mary in English).

Tan-y-bwlch Station (400 yards)

Coed Hafod-y-llyn ❶

Llyn Mair

¼ mile

➤ From car park cross the road and go through gate opposite.
➤ Follow forest track to the **right** of lake and picnic area into trees.
➤ Wind your way for 600 yards to a prominent fork.

❶ ➤ Branch **right** on wider track climbing through woods.
➤ Later, it crosses the Ffestiniog Railway and angles **right** to a junction.

🚂 Ffestiniog Railway

The walk meets the Ffestiniog Railway at a couple of crossings. You may have even arrived by a narrow-gauge train at Tan-y-bwlch Station. Like many of Wales' little steam railways, the Ffestiniog was built initially to serve industry. From 1836 its steam engines brought a substantial tonnage of slate down the mountains from the vast works of Blaenau Ffestiniog on their way to Porthmadog.

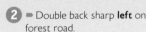

🚂 Ffestiniog Railway   ②   The Oakeleys ☆   ③

| ½ mile | ¾ mile

②
- Double back sharp **left** on forest road.
- On reaching a crossroads climb **right** along another forest road.
- In about 250 yards watch for a grassy path forking **left** to metal gates.

③
- Follow this to an open grassy area below a cottage.
- Go **right** here along a track trending left round the hillside.
- Pass **left** of a cottage's drive; the track snakes down to meet the railway.

NATURE NOTES

The woods were originally known for their sessile oak but in the late 1960s many acres were planted with conifers such as spruce. The Woodland Trust is now thinning these out, removing the invasive rhododendrons and replanting the broadleaved trees.

The woods have been designated as an Area of Conservation for the habitat provides perfect conditions for mosses, liverworts and lichens, as well as rare bats – the lesser horseshoe bat has its European stronghold in the forest.

The rare pine marten also thrives here. This chestnut-coloured stoat-like creature with a pale yellow bib, feeds on small rodents, eggs, insects and fruit. It makes cat-like shrieks and is a very agile climber.

Among the birds you might see are pied flycatchers, redstarts and wood warblers.

Redstart

Left: liverwort
Right: lichens

Ffestiniog Railway

1 mile

1¼ miles

4

4 ➤ Cross the railway line.
➤ Keep **ahead** through trees to next junction.

5 ➤ Keep **left** at the next junction – go round a forest barrier if closed.
➤ Walk to next junction in 100 yards.

Pine marten

Above:
lesser horseshoe bat
Below: wood warbler

Rhododendrons

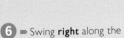

1½ miles

1¾ miles

Tan-y-bwlch Station
(400 yards)
Llyn Mair

6 ➡ Swing **right** along the
grassier track.
➡ It goes on to curve right
and to take you back to **1**.
➡ Turn **right** and retrace
steps back to the start.

Sessile oak

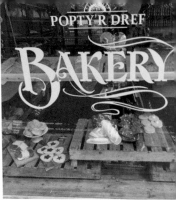

Opposite (clockwise):
Llandudno Pier Ice
Cream & Milkshakes;
Big Rock café and
bakery, Porthmadog.
This page (clockwise):
The Oakeley Arms,
Tan-y-bwlch; Popty'r
Dref bakery and tea
rooms, Dolgellau;
Conwy mussels;
Mary Bellas Café,
Trefriw; The Last Inn,
Barmouth.

FALAFEL
HIGH-SIDER
loaded bottle with salad
and chickpea falafel in
pitta with tahini, lime
and yogurt sauce
£7

VEGETABLE
TWO BEAN CHILLI
JACKET POTATO
with chunky chimichurri
and vinegar slaw
£6.00

MEATBALL
BALONEY:
a baloney big day bun
with meatballs and tomato
tomato-fix gratin
and spinach
£7.00

Sausage
Rolls Royce
New york deli style
with Pork, prawn dijonard
& yellow mustard
relish £3.

GOATS CHEESE
& cranberry
Jacket T- with
toasted goaty toaster
& sea onions
£7.00

THIS IS BIG ROCK

you're WELCOME to join us for
tea, coffee, cake & a deli
house sausage roll this is the
home of THE UNDERGROUND BAKERY

for BREAKFAST, brunch, lunch
bloomers & coffee CAMMED UP

order from the Serve-
like our BIG ROCK
window

The
BIG
ROCK
café

The
UNDERGROUND
BAKERY
at BIG ROCK

all day
BREAKFAST
ROLLS £4.50

COVID
RESTRICTIONS
APPLY -

BORTH-Y-GEST &

PORTHMADOG

This fascinating walk discovers Porthmadog the secret way, over a headland guarding the beautiful bay of Borth-y-Gest, through a tree- and cliff-lined passage past old boatyards. It leads to an ingenious causeway known as the Cob, built by William Madocks. Tremadog Bay and the salt marshes of the Glaslyn and Dwyryd estuaries attract many seabirds, and the return to Borth is highlighted by lofty views over the harbour to the rugged and knolled Rhinog Mountains above Harlech.

Distance	2.8 miles/4.6 km
Time	1½ hours
Start/Finish	Borth-y-Gest
Parking LL49 9TT	Borth-y-Gest car park
Public toilets	Borth-y-Gest car park; Stryd Fawr (High St), Porthmadog
Cafés/pubs	Borth-y-Gest; Porthmadog
Terrain	Lane, pavement, and tarred and gravel paths
Hilliness	Two climbs
Footwear	Year round

Did you know? The poet Shelley was enthusiastic about proposals by William Madocks for the Glaslyn Estuary and the building of a new town at Tremadoc – the latter never got beyond the initial stages and Tremadoc remains a village to this day, even though it has a town hall. It was also the birthplace of TE Lawrence – of Arabia fame – in 1888.

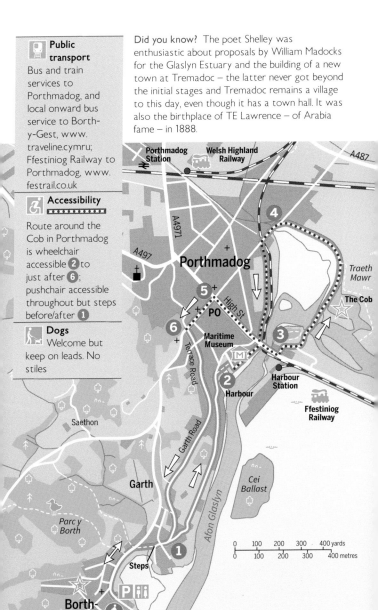

STORIES BEHIND
THE WALK

☆ **Borth-y-Gest** Borth-y-Gest is just a mile from the centre of Porthmadog but it might as well be another world. The headland between them and the rocky hill, Moel-y-Gest, on the other side shuts out the hustle and bustle of its larger neighbour, leaving a small tranquil bay and the colourful houses in relative peace. Before the building of the Cob, Borth-y-Gest was a major crossing point over the sands of the Glaslyn Estuary, Traeth Mawr. Locals would earn money by guiding visitors safely across the treacherous sands.

☆ **The Cob** At the turn of the 19th century Porthmadog was a small village, but that changed in 1808 when William Madocks built a sea wall, the Cob, across the Glaslyn Estuary to reclaim land for farming. Fields were formed replacing the estuary's waters all the way back to the Aberglaslyn Gorge, 5 miles north of Porthmadog. The town grew with the industry that followed and Stryd Fawr (High Street) and the streets about it were built on the newly reclaimed land.

Borth-y-Gest
☆
① Steps   ½ mile ¦
                                              Porthma
                                              Harbo

➡ Bear **right** out of car park to walk along seafront pavement.
➡ At its end fork **right** on a tarred path towards the headland.
➡ Climb 24 steps and keep **forward** as two streets join from the right.

① ➡ At next junction/footpath signpost fork **right**.
➡ Descend lane, then follow signed path down behind the boatyards of Porthmadog to reach harbour.

☆ Shipping and Slate

The newly diverted river scoured out a natural harbour and soon wharves were constructed enabling ocean-going vessels to dock at Porthmadog. In 1836 the Ffestiniog Railway opened and brought slate down from Blaenau Ffestiniog. By 1873 over 117,000 tons were shipped to ports all over the world. At this time shipbuilding had started here. Porthmadog was known especially for its three-masted schooners.

☆ Tourism: Maritime
Museum After World War I the market for slate declined, as did Porthmadog's viability as a port. But the coming of the railways brought tourists and Porthmadog was transformed once more. The town's location makes it an ideal base for exploring Snowdonia and the Lleyn Peninsula, while the Maritime Museum tells the story of the town's quaysides and boat-building history.

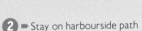

Maritime Museum 🏛 Ffestiniog Railway 🚂 Harbour Station The Cob ☆

3 1 mile Traeth Mawr

2 ➡ Stay on harbourside path to High Street.
➡ Cross the road and the narrow-gauge railway then turn **right** towards the causeway (the Cob).

3 ➡ Turn **left** by Cob Records and follow tarred path which turns **right** then **left** and goes over a tightly enclosed steel bridge to join the Cob.
➡ Follow this round the water to reach a lane.

Walk 8 Borth-y-Gest and Porthmadog   65

NATURE NOTES

The Glaslyn Estuary and Tremadog Bay are wonderful places to see migrating birds such as curlew, oystercatcher and redshank.

In summer there are flocks of sandwich tern, a large white-grey bird with a black-capped head and yellow-tipped black beak.

Ospreys were driven to the brink of extinction in Britain by the early 1900s as, like some other birds of prey, they were shot or poisoned. As you round the Cob and look up to the skies above Traeth Mawr you may be lucky enough to spot one or more. There's a hide at Pont Croesor so you can get a closer look.

Top: treecreeper
Above: grey squirrel
Right: wigeon

1½ miles   Superstore   2 miles

4   High Street   5   Post Office   6   Terrace R

4 ➤ Bear **left** along lane then **left** again alongside the railway track.
➤ This leads past a car park and superstore to High Street.
➤ Go **right**; continue to crossroads in 300 yards.

5 ➤ Turn **left** immediately after post office along street signed to Borth-y-Gest.
➤ Walk to Terrace Road (second left).

Top right: greenshank
Top left: sandwich tern
Left: osprey

Garth Road

Borth-y-Gest ☆

2½ miles | Steps

6 ➤ Turn left. This becomes Garth Road and climbs high above the harbour.
➤ Remain with it to rejoin the outward route at 1.
➤ Descend steps and retrace route back to Borth-y-Gest.

Leatherback sea turtles arrive from the tropics to feast on the jellyfish of Borth-y-Gest and Tremadog Bay during the summer months. This endangered species, unlike other turtles, has a leathery skin rather than a bony shell. It can grow up to a couple of yards long and weigh up to 1,300lbs.

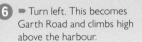

DOLGELLAU: THE MAWDDACH TRAIL

This easy-paced stroll begins alongside the riverside recreation ground known locally as the Marian. The river by your side is the Wnion, which has flowed down from the Aran mountains. Entering the marshy valley of the Mawddach, the track eases across wetlands until it comes to Penmaenpool, with its little signal box/information centre, a fine wooden toll bridge and the welcoming George III Inn – a splendid place for some refreshment before the bus ride back to Dolgellau.

Distance	2.4 miles/3.8km
Time	1¼ hours
Start	Dolgellau Bridge
Finish	Penmaenpool
Parking	LL40 1DL The Marian car park, Dolgellau
Public toilets	The Marian short-stay car park, Dolgellau; by the toll bridge, Penmaenpool
Cafés/pubs	Dolgellau; George III Inn, Penmaenpool
Terrain	Well-surfaced tracks
Hilliness	Level throughout
Footwear	Year round

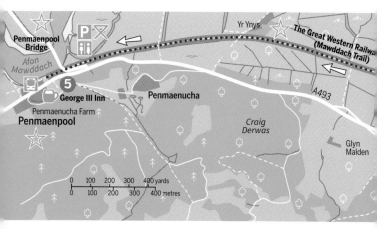

Did you know? George Fox, the prominent Quaker, visited Dolgellau in 1657. Many locals were converted to Quakerism. Some of them were among those who emigrated to Pennsylvania in 1686, under the leadership of Rowland Ellis, a local farmer. His house, Bryn Mawr, gave its name to a town in Pennsylvania.

Did you know? In Welsh mythology, Cadair Idris was part of the hunting grounds of Gwyn ap Nudd, Lord of the Celtic Underworld. It is said he had a pack of strange, red-eared dogs, 'not of this world'. Anyone who heard the howls of these dogs would die and their souls would be herded into the underworld.

 Public transport
Two-hourly bus service from Penmaenpool back to Dolgellau, www. traveline.cymru

Accessibility
Wheelchair and pushchair accessible throughout

Dogs
Welcome but keep on leads due to shared-use cycle path. No stiles

STORIES BEHIND
THE WALK

☆ **The Great Western Railway Line** The Mawddach Trail follows the line of the Great Western Railway, which came from Ruabon via Dolgellau, Corwen and Bala and joined the Cambrian Coast line from Barmouth Junction. It was closed in the 1960s as part of the infamous Beeching Axe.

☕ **George III Inn** The fine 17th-century George III Inn was once a ships' chandler as well as a pub. Today, it's a superb hotel and restaurant. The famous poet Gerard Manley Hopkins penned his poem, *Penmaen Pool* in the inn's guest book.

☆ Dolgellau
☆ Dolgellau Bridge

☆ **M a w d d a c h T r a i l**

The Marian
1½ mile

🚶 🅿 🚻

➡ Start from Dolgellau Bridge (Pont Fawr), adjacent to the Marian short-stay car park. (From the long-stay car park, walk back along road to bridge.)
➡ Follow the tarred track signed Mawddach Trail, initially next to riverside wall, on right-hand side of recreation ground to a footbridge.

1 ➡ Turn **right** over bridge.
➡ Then go **left** along track following the opposite river bank for ½ mile to road bridge.

☆ **Dolgellau** Dolgellau today is a splendid town built from stone and slate and dominated by Gau Crag, the last buttress of the Cadair Idris range. Although Roman coins have been found, there was no significant settlement here until the 12th century, for the lands were marshy. The original church was established at this time, as was Cwmer Abbey, an important religious centre. The stone bridge dates back to 1638 and the current church of St Mary was built in 1716. The town grew from the profits of the wool trade but in the early 19th century Dolgellau also profited from a gold rush. Five hundred people worked the gold mines at nearby Bontddu in the Rhinog hills and Ganllwyd on the Mawddach.

☆ **Penmaenpool** Penmaenpool, at the end of the walk, was built as an estate village for Penmaenuchaf Hall and a ship-building centre. The Grade II-listed wooden toll bridge was constructed in 1879 to replace a ferry crossing. Tragically, 15 people lost their lives in 1966 when the *Prince of Wales* ferry, on a pleasure trip from Barmouth, crashed into the bridge and sank. There's a memorial by the signal box.

☆ **M a w d d a c h   T r a i l**

Afon Wnion · 1 mile · 2 🚗 3 🅿 4

2 ➡ Cross main road (A493) diagonally **right** to waterworks entrance, still following Mawddach Trail.

3 ➡ Go past a car park and keep **forward** to next bridge.

NATURE NOTES

The Afon (river) Wnion, which the route traces out of Dolgellau to its confluence with the Mawddach, is a fine source of sea trout and salmon, which come to spawn in the summer.

Penmaenpool, a Site of Special Scientific Interest, is a valuable breeding area for wetland birds such as redshank and merganser. You may well see buzzard and raven in the skies while cormorant stand and wait for their fish supper on the river.

On the sides of the track below the trees you'll see the hard fern, an evergreen fern that can grow 18-24 inches tall. It is an indicator of ancient woodland and has been used for centuries as an alternative medicine for treating stomach and lung disorders.

Above: sea trout
Right: salmon fry with parr marks
Opposite: merganser, raven, hard fern

Waterworks   1½ miles

☆ The Great Western Railway

4 ➨ Continue on the tree-lined Mawddach Trail embanked above fields, wetland and salt marsh for just over 1 mile to toll bridge in Penmaenpool.

5 ➨ Stroll **forward** a few yards and George III Inn is on **left**.
➨ The bus stop for return to Dolgellau is above George III Inn on the main road.

Buzzard

Penmaenpool

Penmaenpool Bridge
(Afon Mawddach)

2 miles

☆ The Great Western Railway George III Inn

Cormorants

Cormorants are large, black birds with a long neck, webbed feet and hooked beaks. They are superbly fast divers and have been known to reach depths of over 40 feet. They are very successful at catching small- to medium-sized fish.

GO BY STEAM TRAIN
CATCH A FERRY

BARMOUTH TO FAIRBOURNE

A Victorian resort built into the rocks, Barmouth is blessed with wonderful sands and grand views across the Mawddach Estuary to the Cadair Idris mountain range, a view William Wordsworth described as sublime. The bridge across the estuary is ½ mile long. It gives truly memorable views along the estuary and of the mountains either side. Take binoculars as the Mawddach is a haven for wading birds. The little seaside resort of Fairbourne still feels like it's in the 1950s. There is a small toll to cross Barmouth Bridge.

Distance	3.5 miles/5.6km
Time	2 hours
Start Barmouth **Finish** Fairbourne Station	
Parking LL42 1NG Promenade car park, Beach Road	
Public toilets Promenade, Barmouth; Morfa Mawddach Station near ❸; Fairbourne Station	
Cafés/pubs Barmouth; Fairbourne	
Terrain Pavement; wooden boards on bridge; smooth, gravelled path	
Hilliness Generally flat; ascent from Barmouth Harbour; descent to Barmouth Bridge	
Footwear Year round	

Local legend It is said that anyone who gets benighted or spends the night on the mountaintops of Cadair Idris, which looks across the estuary to Barmouth, will return a madman or woman or a poet. The author has and he hasn't written any poetry yet!

Public transport

Train and bus services operate to Barmouth and Fairbourne, www.traveline.cymru For return (seasonal) take Fairbourne Railway to passenger ferry terminal, then ferry to Barmouth Harbour, www. fairbournerailway.com

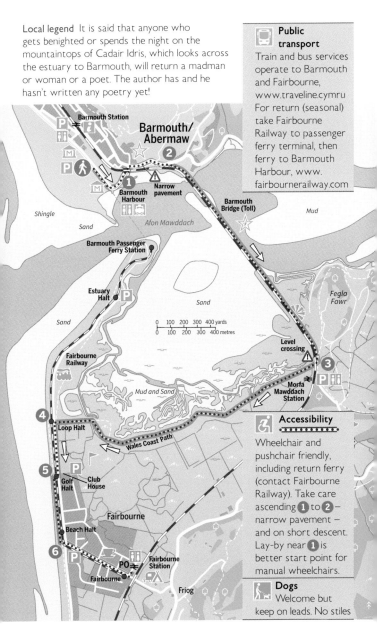

Barmouth Station

Barmouth/ Abermaw 2

1 Barmouth Harbour

⚠️ Narrow pavement

Barmouth Bridge (Toll)

Shingle

Sand

Afon Mawddach

Mud

Barmouth Passenger Ferry Station

Estuary Halt P

Sand

Sand

0 100 200 300 400 yards
0 100 200 300 400 metres

Fairbourne Railway

Mud and Sand

Fegla Fawr

Level crossing ⚠️ 3

Morfa Mawddach Station P

4 Loop Halt

Wales Coast Path

5 Golf Halt P Club House

Fairbourne

Beach Halt

6 P

PO 🚻 Fairbourne Station

Fairbourne

Friog

Accessibility

Wheelchair and pushchair friendly, including return ferry (contact Fairbourne Railway). Take care ascending 1 to 2 – narrow pavement – and on short descent. Lay-by near 1 is better start point for manual wheelchairs.

Dogs

Welcome but keep on leads. No stiles

STORIES BEHIND THE WALK

☆ **Barmouth** Y Bermo, or Barmouth as it is known today, used to be a seaport, trading the woollen goods of Merionydd with the Americas. In those early days there was little space to squeeze in the main road from Harlech, so the houses were built on the cliffs and the road by-passed the village and climbed inland, over the Rhinog mountain passes. In the mid 19th century that changed with the building of a road across the sand. And then the railway came in 1867. Victorian tourists flocked to the seaside and Barmouth prospered.

☆ **Barmouth Bridge**
Barmouth Bridge, completed in 1867, is the longest timber viaduct in Wales. It used to have a swing-bridge section to let tall ships through but it wasn't used for many years and hasn't been operable since the 2021 refurbishment.

Barmouth Station
⇌ (400 yards)   **Barmouth**
                  ☆ Harbour   ❶   narrow pavement   ❷   ☆ **B a r m o u t**

P

½ mile

A f o n   M a w d d a c

➡ Cross the car park to the promenade. Facing the sea, turn **left**.
➡ Walk along promenade, pass Harbourmaster's Office and under railway bridge to road junction.

❶ ➡ Turn **right** on main road pavement, taking care as pavement narrows beneath rocky slopes.
➡ Rise to signed descent to Barmouth Bridge.

🚂 Fairbourne Railway

The steam railway linking Fairbourne with Penrhyn Point dates back to 1895 when Arthur McDougall, of McDougall's flour fame, built it for horse-drawn trams. These were used to transport materials for the construction of Fairbourne village. In 1916 it was converted to 15-inch gauge for use by steam trains. It was closed in 1940 but re-opened in 1947.

☆ **The resort that never happened** Beneath the craggy knoll of Fegla Fawr at the far end of Barmouth Bridge there's a single terrace of houses known as Mawddach Crescent. The houses were built in 1902 by businessman Solomon Andrews as part of an ambitious but ill-fated project to create a holiday resort to rival Barmouth. Unfortunately, the surrounding land proved to be unsuitable for further construction.

r i d g e   Fegla Fawr   🏠 🅿 ⇌ **Morfa Mawddach Station** (120 yards)

| 1 mile | 1½ miles |

2 ▪ Take it **right** down to bridge and pass through gate.
▪ Pay toll and stride out on long timber pathway to the far side of estuary.
▪ Through another gate the path continues by railway past rocky knoll of Fegla Fawr.

3 ▪ On the approach to Morfa Mawddach Station turn **right** through gates and across the railway onto a gravel path topping grassy flood banks.
▪ Follow this (also the Wales Coast Path) all the way to Loop Halt on Fairbourne Railway.

NATURE NOTES

Arthog Bog, just a short distance off route at Morfa Mawddach Station, is an RSPB reserve with a wide variety of plants such as marsh marigold and yellow flag in the spring and hemp agrimony, meadowsweet, ragged robin, bog bean and greater spearwort through the summer. Among the birds you might see here are whitethroat, garden warbler and blackcap.

On the salt marshes between the bridge and Fairbourne you'll see waders such as redshank and oystercatcher foraging in the pools and mud banks. You'll almost certainly see or hear raven (listen for its throaty 'cronk' call) on the rocks of Ynysgyffylog not far from the start of the flood-bank path.

Above: bog bean
Left: ragged robin

2 miles   2½ miles

Wales Coast Path

4 ➡ Here, turn **left** along the road as far as Golf Halt, the next station, in 400 yards.

5 ➡ Opposite the clubhouse veer **right** to join a path by the sea walls.
➡ Just beyond Beach Halt turn **left** to re-cross railway back to road at a junction.

Above: blackcap (male)
Top left: meadowsweet
Left: garden warblers

🚂 F a i r b o u r n e   R a i l w a y

🚂 Loop Halt   🚂 Golf Halt   Beach Halt 🚂   Fairbourne Station 🚂

4 ••••••••••••••• 5 •••••••••••••••••••••• 6 ••••••••••••••••••••••••••••

🚩 🅿 ¦ 3 miles   🅿   3½ miles

6 ➡ Follow road inland past Penrhyn Amusements, a café and a hotel to railway station.

Gorse
Common gorse is quite prolific on the salt marshes. It's a rugged evergreen that flowers between January and June. Small birds take shelter in dense gorse bushes as they provide great protection during harsh weather. The beautifully perfumed flowers are a plentiful source of nectar for bees and butterflies.

Walk 10 Barmouth to Fairbourne   79

Publishing information

© Crown copyright 2022.
All rights reserved.

Ordnance Survey, OS, and the OS logos are registered trademarks, and OS Short Walks Made Easy is a trademark of Ordnance Survey Ltd.

© Crown copyright and database rights (2022) Ordnance Survey.

ISBN 978 0 319092 32 3
1st edition published by Ordnance Survey 2022.

www.ordnancesurvey.co.uk

While every care has been taken to ensure the accuracy of the route directions, the publishers cannot accept responsibility for errors or omissions, or for changes in details given. The countryside is not static: hedges and fences can be removed, stiles can be replaced by gates, field boundaries can alter, footpaths can be rerouted and changes in ownership can result in the closure or diversion of some concessionary paths. Also, paths that are easy and pleasant for walking in fine conditions may become slippery, muddy and difficult in wet weather.

If you find an inaccuracy in either the text or maps, please contact Ordnance Survey at os.uk/contact.

A catalogue record for this book is available from the British Library.

Milestone Publishing credits

Author: John Gillham

Series editor: Kevin Freeborn

Maps: Cosmographics

Design and Production: Patrick Dawson, Milestone Publishing

Printed in Malta by Gutenberg Press

MIX
Paper from responsible sources
FSC® C022612
www.fsc.org

Photography credits

Front cover: Adrian Baker/Shutterstock.com. **Back cover** cornfield/Shutterstock.com.

All photographs supplied by the author ©John Gillham except pages 6 Ordnance Survey; 41 Kevin Freeborn.

The following images were supplied by Shutterstock.com: page 1 Helen Hotson; 16 Ascannio; 16, 44 travellight; 17 AJE44; 18 Halyna Nechyporuk; 19 artel-Artyom Minasyan; 19 Edita Medeina; 19 Mariola Anna S; 19 Menno Schaefer; 24 Krumpelman Photography; 25 arman6732; 25 COULANGES; 25 Yana Fefelova; 25 zakharov aleksey; 33, 79 Andrew M. Allport; 33 Silva Vaughan-Jones; 33, 67 Simonas Minkevicius; 38 Gail Johnson; 38 HTU; 38 Sam Warrenger; 39 Martin Hibberd; 39 RWegmann; 40 Abinieks; 40 Pavel_Voitukovic; 40 SP Wildlife Photography; 40 WildMedia; 41 BBlock; 41 shawnwil23; 46, 59 Erni; 46 Karel Bock; 47 Colin Seddon; 47 Jenny Cottingham; 52 bearacreative; 52 Sandra Standbridge; 52 Skrypnykov Dmytro; 53 Martin Fowler; 53 Paul Abrahams; 53 Ryzhkov Sergey; 58 HAOS; 58 Przemyslaw Muszynski; 58 Zeno Swijtink; 59 Anatoliy Vlasov; 59 Djohan Shahrin; 59 Mark Caunt; 59 Okyela; 60 Alex Staroseltsev; 65 DANIEL NORRIS; 66 Kemaro; 66 LecartPhotos; 66 Nora Yero; 67 Dennis Jacobsen; 67 Speyside snaps; 67 William Farah; 72 Kletr; 72 Marek Rybar; 73 Piotr Krzeslak; 73 Susan Hodgson; 73 WaceQ; 78 Aleksandra Duda; 78 Graeme Dawes; 78 Maximillian cabinet; 79 SHARKY PHOTOGRAPHY; 79 Wirestock Creators.